NANCY KERRIGAN:
In My Own Words

NANCY KERRIGAN:
In My Own Words

Nancy Kerrigan with Steve Woodward

Hyperion Paperbacks for Children
New York

First Hyperion Paperback edition 1996
1 3 5 7 9 10 8 6 4 2

The text for this book is set in 12-point Adobe Minion.

Designed by Impress, Inc.

Library of Congress Catalog Card Number: 95-81906

ISBN: 0-7868-1042-4 (paperback)

Foreword

THIS BOOK describes the experiences of a skinny young girl from Massachusetts who grew up wearing ice skates. This is my story, from that first skating lesson in 1975 to the final dramatic night of the Winter Olympics in 1994. In between were chilly New England mornings at the rink, a lot of stumbles and tumbles, exciting trips and new skating friends, disappointments and victories.

As a skater, I've won dozens of medals. My name is recorded as a U.S. champion and twice as an Olympian. But my life growing up was very routine. I'd get up in the morning, skate, go to school, skate some more, come home and do homework, watch a little TV, and go to bed. Doesn't sound too exciting, does it?

But that was the basis for everything that came later. I won medals because of some natural talent, some luck, and being in the right place at the right time—plus a lot of hard work.

Maybe you've found something you can do well, something you enjoy doing almost every day, just as I did with skating. Success as an athlete, artist, musician—or whatever you might choose to be—takes time, patience, and courage. Your friends might think you're different—and you might think so, too. I sure did. But if you believe in yourself and follow your heart, you will find the courage to keep going. And you will succeed, which to me means being happy with yourself for trying to be *your* best.

Chapter 1

I DON'T KNOW why I became a figure skater. I didn't know when I was six, taking my first lessons. And even now I can't find the words to explain why I loved the sport so much from the time I first stepped on the ice. One thing is certain: It never was about wanting to go to the Olympics, winning a medal, or becoming famous.

I was a tomboy who wanted to do exactly what my two older brothers did. Mark is five years older than me; Michael is three years older. And all I wanted in life was to be cool--just like them. I wore jeans and a green sweatshirt to look more like one of the guys. I still remember my excitement the Christmas when we all got hockey sticks. And since Mark and Michael played ice hockey constantly, I wanted to play, too. Maybe that's what got me interested in figure skating—that and the jumping! I loved to jump, and I loved the energy of skating fast to music.

I started skating by taking group lessons. Once a week, I'd have an hour-long class with about twenty other kids. We'd have a lesson for half an hour, then spend the rest of the time practicing what we'd learned and playing.

The first thing we learned was how to stand up with skates on, keeping our feet together and bending a little bit at the knees for balance. After we got enough confidence to move forward on skates, we found out that it's not easy to stop. So we were taught how to put one foot slightly out to the side and make a little pile of "snow." Then we started skating in little circles, trying to become comfortable with the ice beneath the blades. I moved along pretty quickly in those first group lessons and discovered in no time that I liked going fast. Falling down didn't bother me at all—I just popped right back up. It was standing still that got on my nerves.

About two years later, I switched to private lessons with Theresa Martin, who was my coach the first nine years of my skating career in my hometown of Stoneham, Massachusetts. Theresa told my parents that she thought I had the potential to be better than a group lesson skater and that she'd like to teach me. After some semiprivate lessons with three other kids, I moved on to one-on-one lessons with Theresa.

As you can imagine, my brothers were thrilled when I started taking all those figure-skating lessons. They thought that meant I was less likely to hang around when they were trying to play with their friends.

To their dismay, I *still* loved playing street hockey and tagged along whenever I could. Once my brothers figured out I wasn't going away, they finally let me into some of their games. But they made me play goalie, probably because they figured I'd get scared and quit. That was a big mistake. Any time they told me I couldn't do something, I just had to try to prove them wrong.

I'd put on those big, heavy pads and an old goalie mask, the kind that fits tight against your face. If the hockey puck hits you right on the mask, it still hurts. But I stood right in front of the goalie's box and let them fire away. I loved every minute, except for those shots from about ten feet away. Those *could* scare me—a lot! My brothers were older and obviously stronger. Sometimes I ended up with black eyes, but I thought that was cool.

I wanted to please my brothers so much that I even started to think like a hockey player. I'd go to my lesson, put my skates on, and race out on the ice, bent over and going as fast as I could from one end of the rink to the other. After warming up, I'd start doing my jumps from a hockey player's crouched stance. Theresa, my coach, just shook her head.

"OK, Nancy," she said. "Now go back and do it again. And this time stand up *straight*."

"Figure skating is for wimps," I announced, repeating what my brothers always told me. "I don't want to do it like that."

By the end of my lesson, Theresa usually had convinced me that figure skaters are not hockey players and vice versa. Then I'd go home and my brothers would start all over again:

"It's for wimps."

For a while, I didn't know who to believe, but I was determined to continue skating and soon decided to ignore my brothers. I think you quickly discover how much you enjoy a sport or other activity by the way you react to what others say about it. My brothers still gave me a hard time—all in good fun—and some of my friends didn't understand why I wanted to skate almost every day, but their opinions never changed my mind.

Even at six or seven years old, I wanted to try the jumps. It didn't matter to me that I had never done them before. I had a strong feeling, a belief that I could do all the jumps before I ever tried them.

When I watched skating on TV, I usually enjoyed the men's skating much more than the women's. As a tomboy, I thought of myself as rough and tough, so I liked the athletic part of skating, especially the jumping. When I was a young girl in the mid-1970s, most of the jumping was done by the men. The women were just starting to add more difficult jumps to their programs, but it was nothing like it was by the time I reached the senior level in the late 1980s.

One skater who made a real impression on me was a jumping master named Mark Cockerall, a member of the 1984 U.S. Olympic skating team. He was one of the first skaters in the world who could do two triple jumps in a row, also called a triple-triple combination.

This combination is quite hard to do correctly. At that time, you only saw one if you were watching men's skating. Women were doing triple-into-double combinations, but not triple-triples.

Still, I decided I wanted to do one just the way Mark Cockerall did. So I went to work on a triple toe loop, triple toe loop combination. First, you take off into the triple toe loop, spinning around three times in the air. You land on one foot and the use the same foot to take off for the next triple toe loop, spinning three more times.

I was only about fourteen when I started practicing this combination, so I had plenty of time on my side. As usual, I was impatient. When I gave myself a goal, I felt like I had to achieve it *right then*. After about one week of practice, I landed my very first triple-triple. It felt great. I wanted to do it again and again after that, and I did.

When I competed as a novice at fifteen, I planned to do a triple-triple at the beginning of my long program, but I got nervous and left it out. Later in the routine, I looked at my coach questioningly: *Should I try it?* She shrugged and nodded, so I took off—and landed the jump at the end of my program.

After the competition, some of the judges were saying, "Wow, that was great! Who is this skater?" I was fifteen years old, but I looked about eleven, and no one had ever heard of me. Other judges were saying, "Did I see what I thought I saw?" Most men weren't landing triple-triples, no other women were landing them—and I was only at the novice level. It was so unexpected that I don't think a lot of people realized what had happened.

I was beginning to realize I wasn't just an average figure skater. But I also knew I had a lot more work ahead of me.

Chapter 2

SKATING WAS never an obsession at my house. Some parents or coaches think talented young skaters should be tutored at home or take correspondence classes, which means doing homework but never going to a classroom with other kids. I'm not sure that's a good idea. I went to school with other kids every day, so I always had the chance to look around and see the world outside the ice rink.

However, I did pay a price. Depending on when my lessons were scheduled, I sometimes was allowed to come to school later in the morning or leave a little early. I didn't always have to go to music or gym classes so I could get to practice on time. That may sound great, but it was hard making new friends because I was always going to practice when they were doing other things.

Plus, when I'd come to school late, I'd usually walk into the middle of a lesson. I was always trying to catch up with what was going on and the other kids would look at me and say, "Hey, why does *she* get to come late?"

I felt very isolated, but I did a lot of that to myself. I decided that no one would like me and became quite shy. Then other kids would think, Well, she must be a snob or something—but I was just scared to open my mouth.

Sometimes in high school, I would say hi to someone and she would talk to me because no one else was around. Then a group of kids would come around the corner and the person I was talking to would ignore me. Now I realize that no one meant to hurt my feelings; they just wanted to fit in themselves. At the time, though, I felt that I was odd and that I'd never belong.

Luckily, I was able to talk to my mom about the way I felt. She pointed out that, although she still kept in touch with several high school friends, most people don't. They move on with their lives and make new friends in college; then they start families and make new friends in their neighborhoods. I thought about that for a while and decided that I wasn't willing to give up a sport that I loved just to be more social—especially since my social groups were going to keep changing as I grew up.

So even though I felt like an outcast sometimes and there were days when I came home and cried a lot, year after year, I decided to stick with skating.

I think many girls who are good athletes quit sports in junior high for two reasons. The first is simple biology: When you go through puberty, your body changes and you gain some weight. It can be frustrating because you have to adjust to a new height, a new weight, and a new body shape. I know that when I developed hips, my rotation in the air changed when I did jumps and I suddenly couldn't do the triples that I had been easily landing before. I had to relearn skills, often going back to basics, and that was hard. But if you love your sport, it's definitely worth it!

The second is also simple biology, and it can be summed

up in one word: *boys*. A lot of girls are afraid that boys won't like them if they're athletic. That thought went through my mind as well when I was growing up . . . but then I realized that I probably wasn't going to marry that twelve-year-old boy that I thought was so cute. So why should I give up my skating for him?

Perhaps having few friends as a kid helped bring me even closer to my family. I certainly had enough family in the area. When I was growing up, there must have been ninety-five or more people from both sides of my family living in Stoneham or the other little towns nearby. Until they passed away, my grandparents lived down the street, just two houses away from ours. My dad was raised with eight brothers and sisters, many of whom also lived in the area.

(My brothers and I are continuing the tradition of sticking close by. All three of us recently married. My husband and I live eight miles from my parents' house—and both my brothers live between ten and fifteen minutes away from me.)

With all that family around, I had a great network of support and help in my skating career. My parents, grandparents, and several aunts and uncles all came to my first national championship in Kansas City, Missouri, to cheer me on. Many family members would try to attend other competitions when they could afford to travel. In fact, for years family vacations were planned around skating events—which are not always fun. They can be stressful even for those nervously sitting in the stands and watching. But it helped me a great deal to know that people who loved me had made the effort to be there and support me.

Because skating is such an expensive sport, some family members would help my parents pay for skates or lessons when they could. A lot of times they'd pick me up at school and take me to the rink, which would take a lot of pressure off my dad. During all those years, they kept asking me, "Now, tell me again why you're doing this?" And I kept saying, "I don't know. I just love skating." Then they'd ask my parents the same thing. My parents would say, "We don't know either! It's crazy! But Nancy loves skating and she keeps getting better, so we'll keep at it." Luckily for me, everyone accepted these rather vague answers and kept pitching in when needed.

Of course, the expense of skating meant that I felt pressure to follow through on my end. Through many years of skating lessons, my parents never lectured me about what a great skater I was going to be someday or about how I'd never make the Olympic team if I missed a lesson. But they were perfectly honest in telling me that the lessons already were paid for with money we could not afford to waste just because I was in a bad mood. If my dad paid the coach for ten weeks of lessons, he expected me to keep skating until the ten weeks ended. If I wanted to quit after that, I could.

Sometimes, at five o'clock in the morning, I'd wake up and try to convince myself that I wanted to go back to sleep. Once in a while, my mom would even say, "Go back to sleep if you feel like it."

Then I'd lie in bed and thoughts would start running through my mind: *I love skating. I'll feel guilty if I don't go. We've already paid for the lesson. My coach expects me to be there. If I want to make that goal, I should go. OK, I'm going.*

So I'd get up and my mom, who was already back in bed, would say, "What are you doing?"

"I'm going to the rink."

And she'd sigh and say, "OK. I'll make breakfast."

My first few years of lessons cost more than twenty dollars for an hour, and the price went up from there as I advanced as a skater. By the time I was at the senior level, my family paid about $50,000 a year, which included the costs for lessons, skating boots, choreography, music, travel, and the dresses I wore at competitions.

Sometimes the expenses seemed endless. I would need three or four pairs of skates a year because I was growing or because they would just break down. Each pair could cost $800. Once I got a new pair and almost immediately grew out of them. My parents felt bad about it, but they asked me to wear them as long as I could. We had the leather stretched, but I'd still cry every morning when I stepped on the ice. Ice rinks are freezing and when your feet are squished inside your boots, they're *really* cold. Finally, I got new skates—and found out that I had been skating with boots that were two and a half sizes too small.

When I got older and was winning at a higher level, people started telling us that I needed custom-made skates. We couldn't afford them, but we heard that a girl we knew had just gotten custom-made skates—and then quit skating two weeks later.

We bought the used skates from her without realizing that it wasn't a good idea to skate with boots that had been custom-made to fit someone else's feet. At first, when I practiced with those skates, I'd feel awful pain and the inside of the boots would be red from blood. Eventually, the leather molded to my feet—but for a long time it was hard to believe that those expensive skates were worth the money.

Despite our family's help, a lot of the financial burden for my skating career fell on my dad. He worked at a gelatin plant where he made enough money to give us a nice house, food to eat, and clothes to wear. But there was not a penny to waste, especially when I started skating lessons and had a private coach. We applied for some bank loans and my dad found some other part-time jobs, too. For a few years, he drove a Zamboni, the machine that spreads water on the ice rink to make a smooth layer of ice on top. He would arrive in the morning, open the rink for those with early lessons, including me, and make the ice. In return, we paid less money for my time on the ice.

My dad also worked for a man who owned houses that were rented to other families. When something needed to be repaired, my dad got a phone call. And when a family would move out, he'd go to the house and get it ready for the next renter. He's very good at fixing things, but it was still hard work and long hours.

My mom took care of us and our home, but it was harder for her than for most moms. She lost most of her eyesight in 1970, about one year after I was born. I was too young to know what was happening, of course, but it was a terrible time for our family. A few years before I was born, my mom got sick from a virus that lasted for a long time. Eventually, the virus went away but it left behind a reminder. Very slowly, the nerves around her eyes stopped working, and she had more and more trouble seeing. She isn't completely blind, but everything looks blurred and fuzzy to her.

Since I grew up in a home with a mom who can't see very well, it seemed normal to me. I can't remember anyone ever sitting me down, saying, "Nancy, your mom is blind." But I did have to learn a few things at a much younger age than most kids. I learned how to read a clock and tell time when I was only about four years old. My mom had a hard time with this, especially since back then there were no clocks with bright numbers instead of hands like there are today.

During televised competitions, my mom is often shown sitting with her face close to a TV screen to watch me as I skate. This helps her see me a little more clearly, but she can't see me smile when I land a jump or frown when I fall. After so many years, she knows what's going on just by listening to the crowd and to my dad, who has learned to describe different parts of my performances.

A lot of people feel sorry for my mom because she'll never see me skate as clearly as someone with regular eyesight. But just ask people who know her well and they'll tell you that my mom doesn't want anyone's pity. For one thing, she doesn't feel sorry for herself. She's one of the most determined people I know.

For another thing, people who have one of their senses taken away, like eyesight, often make up for it in other ways. My mom sure did. After meeting people a couple of times, she almost never forgets their voices. That's how she identifies people. And I've always found that she is very "people smart." If somebody is upset and trying to hide it, she figures that out before anyone else does.

After it started to become clear that I had athletic ability, Mark and Michael became two of my earliest fans. But when I was little, they teased me a lot. I went through a long, awkward stage when I was ten to fifteen years old, and Mark had a habit of calling me "Ug"—as in ugly.

But they were always there for me. I even inherited my brothers' paper route when I was eleven or twelve years old. That meant that I could have some spending money without having to ask my parents for it. I'd rush home after school on Thursday afternoons, pick up the papers, and run from one house to another. I had only one hour to deliver them all before my skating lesson. With a little practice I learned all the shortcuts through backyards and woods and got pretty good at it.

Later, I became a waitress at a little restaurant in my hometown. With the money I earned, I could pay for the gas I needed to drive my dad's old Chevrolet Caprice—a big, silver sedan with a few rust spots—to and from skating practice. Sometimes I even had a little left over to spend on clothes.

I probably could have had an easier schedule by getting a job at a local ice rink, but I had been skating for ten years by now and figured that I already spent enough time there. Plus, having a job someplace where people didn't care about skating was a lot of fun. I got to meet new people and make new friends. I felt like I had a real life for a few hours a week.

Compared to the running around I did at work, the skating rink seemed almost peaceful. I think it was then that I realized I was lucky. Lucky that I had the ability to skate and lucky to have the opportunity to keep working and improving.

Chapter 3

I HAD SO MUCH ENERGY when I was little and most of it was in my feet. When I was about four years old, I can remember dancing across the kitchen floor to whatever music was on the radio or television. So when I began taking skating lessons in 1975, the transition from the kitchen to the ice rink seemed easy to me.

However, I soon found out that, as great as it feels to perform a new jump or spin, actually learning that new skill can be frustrating. It takes a lot of determination and discipline to keep going to the rink, even when you feel as if you'll never figure out how to do a lutz without falling.

Sometimes when I got really down about my skating, my mom would remind me, "If you want to quit, you can. It's up to you. If you don't want to skate anymore—"

"No, I *do* want to skate," I'd always say. Then after a minute, I'd realize: "Maybe I just don't want to skate *today.*"

I soon discovered that you have to find a way to make it worth being at the rink, even if you're having a really bad day. You don't want to waste that expensive ice time, but you also have to realize that something is telling you not to push too hard today. When I was feeling burned out, I'd usually play a little bit with my skating friends, just skating around and talking. That wasted some time, but it helped me relax. Then I'd go practice my jumps.

It also helps to smile, even when—maybe *especially* when— you don't feel like it. When I was young, I smiled all the time when I was skating. Then I got older and thought, I can't do that now because I'm skating to more serious music. Besides, if I smile, I'll lose all my energy.

Of course, that was crazy because smiling actually *gives* you energy! I had it all backward. But I finally figured it out, and now I try to smile all the time when I'm performing, even if I'm not happy. I'll think, OK, I just fell, but my arm movements are pretty! And it makes a difference. People in the audience will tell me later, "Who cares if you fell? The routine was beautiful." And when I smile, I don't get upset with myself for falling and I have more fun.

Someone told me that smiling relaxes about two hundred muscles in your body. I don't know if that's true or not, but it feels like it is. Now when I see young skaters getting upset because they're falling on their jumps, I'll say, "Come on, smile. Really, it's going to help."

FINALLY, AFTER YEARS OF LESSONS, I got to enter my very first skating competition, the 1979 Boston Open in Massachusetts. I was just about to turn ten years old and this was my chance to show an audience all I was learning from hours and hours of lessons. By then, I knew how to do a single Axel jump—one and a half turns in the air. None of Theresa's students were allowed to skate a program with music until they could do that Axel consistently. I worked very hard and finally was able to do it most of the time. I showed

Theresa I was ready by landing a single Axel that day in Boston, plus I remember more or less doing everything else in my freestyle program just as I had practiced it. Before I knew it, my performance was over and I was skating off the ice.

I then watched some of the other skaters, but I was getting restless. My skates were off by now, so I decided it was time for me to go. Next thing I knew, I had coaxed some of my skating friends out of the arena and across the street, where we found a park with a great swing set.

The Boston Open went on without me. I was having so much fun on the swings that it surprised me when another skater came running over with some news she thought I needed to know.

"Nancy, you finished second," she said. "You won the silver medal!"

"Great!" I said. "Thanks for telling me." And I went on swinging.

The girl just stood there and looked at me. She seemed puzzled, so I asked what was wrong.

"The medal," she said. "You've got to go back inside and get your medal. Hurry up."

To me, this seemed like bad timing. I was having fun on the swings, and this girl wanted me to go back inside just to get a medal. Eventually, I decided she was right and I walked back to the arena, where my first medal was placed around my neck.

The spectators, including my parents and brothers, were clapping and shouting as the medal winners skated off the ice. I was starting to enjoy myself, too. But then I remembered that my coach, Theresa, had told me that medals are prizes, not jewelry. She believed it was wonderful to win medals, but not to brag about them, and so she told us not to run around wearing them. From that day and for years to come, I was always proud to win a medal but it came off as soon as I left the ice.

The Boston Open gave me a lot of confidence and I continued to skate well and win medals. It seemed like I was always going somewhere for a competition. Even though I wasn't traveling very far from home, places like Providence, Rhode Island, seemed far away to me.

Those trips were tough, because I always got homesick. I'd be at a competition with a big group of people I didn't know and I'd think, I don't know them, they don't know me. They probably don't like me. I realize now that this isn't very logical; those strangers didn't have any reason to dislike me and probably would have been very nice. At the time, however, I couldn't get up the nerve to talk to anybody.

But I really liked the chance to perform and improve, and for four or five years, in events such as the Worcester Open, the Cohasset Open, and others in the area, I was doing both, continuing to move into more advanced levels.

Unlike most other sports, the level at which you compete in skating is not decided by your age but by ability to master certain skills required by the United States Figure Skating Association (USFSA). You move into the next level by passing a "test" of these skills on the ice. The five levels of competition are: juvenile, intermediate, novice, junior, and senior. The only age limits are at the senior level, where you must be at least twelve to compete in an international event (against skaters from other countries) and at least fourteen to skate in the Olympics or World Championships. Coaches typically help skaters decide when it is time to attempt the next test. As if this is not complicated enough, when I was competing, skaters had to pass not one but two tests before advancing. There was a "figures" test and a "free skating" test.

Compulsory school figures are made up of a series of patterns, each traced using the inside or outside "edge" of the right or left skate blade. An edge also is identified by its direction—forward and backward. Free skating, also called freestyle, is the kind you see on television—spins and jumps connected by footwork and set to music. (After 1990, figures no longer were part of competition at the senior level.)

Most kids like skating a program to music because you're going pretty fast. For figures, you go slow and try to be very precise. And there is no music.

I was always bored by figures; I was always looking around when I was supposed to be concentrating on tracing the patterns in the ice. If the door to the rink opened, I'd automatically glance up to see who was coming in. Anything to distract me from practicing. But I loved free skating and I never finished lower than second place in the early years of my career. As much as I disliked the figures, I even won a couple of those medals, too. When I was thirteen, competing as an intermediate, I was gold medalist in both figures and free skating at the New England Regionals.

It was great to win, but I soon found out that skating is more difficult when people expect you to be good every time you compete. I started worrying about this, and my confidence began to wilt. Mostly, I was nervous—too nervous. My legs would shake as I traced my figures in front of the judges or skated to center ice to start my program. The only way I could stop this trembling was to concentrate hard on what I was trying to do on the ice.

When I was thirteen, competing in the Boston Open, I nearly made a big mistake by concentrating too much on one part of a figure that I wanted to do correctly. I ended up facing in the wrong direction because I was thinking only about which edge I was supposed to be using. Before it was too late, my coach Theresa whistled and motioned with her hand to get me to turn around. If she had not stopped me, I doubt the judges would have recognized the figure.

I had another close call at about the same time, when I was almost disqualified for arriving late at the Cohasset Open. I had to change into my skating dress in the car on the way to the rink. When we finally got there, I ran in and saw the girls in my division on the ice, warming up. By the time I put on my skates and laced them up, the warm-up period—usually about five minutes—was over. I was allowed to skate anyway, but I knew I never wanted to go through that kind of panic again. After that, I was always careful about being on time.

In a few more years, I started flying to competitions that were even farther from home. I traveled to Kansas City, Missouri, in 1985 to compete in my first U.S. Championships. I was fifteen, skating in the novice division. I only finished ninth, but it was exciting to be with skaters from all over the country, performing in a big arena.

That was also my first and last year as a pairs skater. I'd decided to try pairs for the 1984–85 season because I thought it would be fun. In Kansas City, I skated in the junior pairs competition with Bobby Martin, Theresa's younger brother. We finished eleventh. It's not unusual for skaters to try skating both singles and pairs, especially when they're younger. But few end up doing both for very long.

A FEW MONTHS AFTER the 1985 Championships, my career went into a period of transition, and I had some major decisions to make. First, I went back to training as a full-time singles skater after Bobby decided to quit pairs for a while. It was also about this time that I started working with Cathy Collins, a ballet, jazz, and tap dance teacher. For about four years, she helped me learn dance steps that I could use in my programs and played an important role in helping me develop my movement over the ice. Cathy taught me a lot about balance, footwork, and control of my body, which helped me be more confident when I skated. Later, she also helped me get into Emmanuel College after high school. Not only did I get a scholarship to help pay for college, but my teachers were very flexible in allowing me time off for skating.

That summer, Theresa suggested I spend a few weeks with another coach, mainly for a change of pace. A lot of young skaters do this, especially in the summer when you tend to train somewhat more intensely.

I went to Denver to work with Don Laws, coach of 1984 Olympic champion Scott Hamilton. That was where I landed those triple-triple jump combinations, and I remember how surprised Scott was when he saw me doing them. He leaned over to Mr. Laws and whispered, "I didn't think girls were doing that yet." Since Scott had won an Olympic gold medal the year before, I was pleased he had noticed me.

Soon after, I returned to Massachusetts, only to be greeted with the news that Theresa and her family were moving to North Carolina. Skaters often move with their coaches, but I wasn't crazy about the idea of living so far away from home. So Theresa introduced my parents and me to Denise Cahill, who coached me in 1986, the first year I skated singles in the junior division.

I was happy with my accomplishments for most of that season. I placed second in the New England Regionals and fourth in the Eastern Sectionals. Those finishes gave me confidence when I competed in my first U.S. Championships as a junior. Unfortunately, I got a little too psyched up, made some mistakes, and finished eleventh.

Later that year, history repeated itself. Denise moved to Baltimore but before she left, she introduced my parents and me to Mary and Evy Scotvold, a husband-and-wife coaching team at the Skating Club of Boston, where I was training. Both are instructors, but Mary also specializes in choreography, which means creating routines to music. Evy specializes in the technical aspects of the sport. Our meeting went well, and I was soon working with Mary and Evy to prepare for the 1986–87 season, my final year as a junior competitor.

This was a major development in my life as a skater. By now, I was a high school senior and had been skating for more than eleven years. I didn't realize it then, but much of what I knew about the sport came from instinct. When I saw Mark Cockerall do that triple-triple combination, it was as if I was able to freeze an image of his jumps in my mind. Then it was just a matter of practicing, falling, and practicing some more until I could do them. The problem with being a "natural skater" was that I didn't always know how to fix a flawed skill.

Mary and Evy wanted to teach me technique. They believe a skater needs to perfect each small part of a spin or a jump before moving on to more difficult skills. When a skater does a jump without falling, it doesn't mean the jump is correct. The body position might be unbalanced or the landing might not be as pretty or graceful as it should be. There are dozens of little things that judges look for when comparing performances between skaters. Mary and Evy felt I could be one of the top skaters in the United States, so they insisted I work on eliminating bad habits.

We argued now and then, but I couldn't complain about the results. I moved up from eleventh to fourth at the 1987 Junior Championships, then passed my senior tests for the 1987–88 season. That 1988 U.S. Championship was a rude awakening to the senior level. I placed twelfth. Instead of being disappointed, I used that experience to motivate myself even more, and I was showing signs of real progress the following season. In the fall of 1988, I won two international competitions—one in Austria, the other in Hungary—and moved all the way up to fifth at the 1989 U.S. Championships in Baltimore, Maryland, the following January.

None of this happened by accident. To be at your best for those few short minutes in front of an audience, you have to devote weeks and months to the inside of a chilly ice rink where the only spectators are other skaters and their coaches.

Making a mark at the senior level is a job; it requires a year-round commitment. Still, you can balance training time with the rest of your life. For a year after high school, I worked and skated an average of sixty to seventy hours a week. The following year, I took courses at Emmanuel College and worked for a year or so stocking merchandise for a discount clothing store. But all of this was squeezed in around trips to the skating rink.

A skating "season" typically begins in September or October and ends in mid-March. Top seniors can expect to be assigned to one or more international invitational competitions, either in the U.S., Canada, or Europe. Also, skaters who don't win medals in the previous year's U.S. Championships must enter regional or sectional qualifying events to earn a chance to compete in the next Championships.

Like most competitive skaters, my preparations for new seasons began during the summer. The first step is finding music to go with the two programs you will perform—a technical, or short, program lasting two minutes, forty seconds; and a free, or long, program lasting four and a half minutes. Every skater has different reasons for selecting music and different ways of looking for it. You have to like your program's music, but it also has to fit your skating style and help you to demonstrate your strengths. Although I sometimes picked music for shows or exhibitions myself, I worked closely with Mary, who spent hours listening to tapes and CDs to decide on music for competition.

After we settle on a piece of music, Mary has it edited to fit the time limits required by international rules. Together, we listen to the edited music and begin designing the choreography. Creating a routine is like sitting down in front of a big stack of puzzle pieces. The idea is to take all of the parts of a skating program—spins, footwork, jumps—and perform them in a way that flows naturally with the music's mood and tempo.

For a short program, you are required to include eight specific elements. The long program rules allow more freedom, but the number of jumps and jump combinations, and the difficulty of the skills you perform, is still important.

To have a program ready for the judges, you constantly make small changes throughout the season. Mary and I have set programs to music in as little as two days. Others have taken as long as a couple of weeks to be put together from start to finish.

After the choreography's complete, there's still more to be done—like picking out a dress. Most nationally ranked skaters use designers. Toward the end of my competitive years, we worked with Vera Wang, who designs beautiful dresses and gowns for actresses and entertainers. We usually sent my music to Vera, who listened to it and then suggested styling and colors that seemed to be the right fit.

Even when you've found the right music, the perfect dress, and a strong program, the fact remains that skating is a sport that requires excellent physical conditioning. No matter how much natural skating ability a person might have, two or three hours a day on the ice is not enough at the senior level. I am an athlete first, a skater second. I worked out regularly in the gym, lifting free weights or using a Nautilus machine to get stronger and build enough stamina to get through one of those four-and-a-half-minute free programs without being exhausted. I also studied ballet and contemporary dance to improve the artistic quality of my performances and studied tap to develop my footwork on the ice.

From year to year, the cycle never seemed to end. But eventually all the hard work began to make a real difference. In 1990, I moved up one spot from the year before and placed fourth at the U.S. Championships in Salt Lake City, Utah.

However, that competition proved to be a turning point for me. I was ranked third in both the short and long programs, which counted for eighty percent of the total score, but I was ranked seventh in figures, which counted for twenty percent of the total. That meant that I ended up fourth—and only the top three medal winners got the chance to compete in the World Championships.

The girl who won third place was fourth or fifth in the free skating programs but had done better than me in figures. I kept saying, "How did this happen? Show me that math again." It was hard to understand how I could be better in the part of the competition that counted the most and still not make the World Championships team.

I realized that I was now as good as the three skaters who

I've loved skating since I was six years old. This is me at twelve years old, practicing at the rink near my home in Massachusetts.

(Above) This is me at three years old with my brothers Mark, who is five years older than me, and Michael, who is three years older. I thought they were totally cool and wanted to be just like them. (Below) Here we are, all grown-up. They're still cool.

My brothers taught me how to play hockey—and how to face a flying puck without flinching.

Here's an early attempt at my extended spiral—on roller skates!

Lacing up for practice. I always wore three or four layers of clothing because it was *sooo* cold. But as I skated and worked up a sweat, the layers were removed.

Here I am with my parents, brothers, and grandmother. When I was growing up, I had about ninety-five family members living nearby.

As I traveled around the world to competitions, I became friends with other skaters. Here I am at the 1992 World Championships (above) with Todd Eldredge, Paul Wiley, and Kristi Yamaguchi and (right) with Brian Boitano from the Campbell's Tour.

ACKERLEY

Congratulations to Stoneham's
Nancy Kerrigan
Winning the Bronze Medal
1992 Winter Olympics

Winning the bronze medal at the 1992 Winter Olympics was a highlight of my career. My hometown of Stoneham, Massachusetts, welcomed me home with a billboard and a parade in my honor.

Believe in Yourself &
Always dream!
Nancy Kerrigan

I love signing autographs. I just wish I could talk to everyone I meet!

had finished ahead of me and won the medals, but I was still bothered by nervousness when the time came to show the judges what I could do.

My friend Paul Wylie said I was paying too much attention to what he called "the voice"—those whispers of self-doubt that creep into your mind when the pressure is on. Paul, who also was coached by Mary and Evy, had been bothered by "the voice" a few times himself, especially in those tense moments right before being called onto the ice. Paul discovered that listening to music through portable headphones helped him relax at competitions and he suggested I do the same.

Perhaps even more importantly, I also realized that I had never really challenged myself to put everything on the line when I competed. For seventeen years, I had only pushed myself halfway—and it had worked, in the sense that I had won medals. But I had never done my *very best*, because that was too scary. What if I wasn't as good as I thought I could be? What if I tried my best and still didn't win?

Finally, I decided that didn't matter. I wanted to be able to say that I had done my best, no matter what the results were.

For the 1990–91 season I developed two new programs— a short program to music arranged by Mark Militano, a former pairs skater, and a long program adapted to a movie soundtrack, *Born on the Fourth of July*. I also began a new type of preparation away from the ice, called stress training. Working with a sports psychologist, I learned how to replace negative thoughts with positive thoughts.

That's harder than it sounds. For years, I would miss one jump or spin and "the voice" would start whispering in my head: *You stink, you can't do this, you're no good.* It was ridiculous, of course, because nobody can be perfect all the time.

And if you're constantly telling yourself you can't do something, guess what—you can't! But after years of thinking this way, it had become a habit that I had to work hard to break.

It was about this time that I also discovered that I had developed another bad habit of holding all my emotions—good or bad—inside. As I was coming up through the ranks, I had learned not to act too happy when I won or too upset when I lost because the judges sometimes took those reactions into consideration at the next competition. Too happy might mean you were bragging; too upset might mean you were a bad sport. So I built a wall around myself to the point that, when I won the Olympic Sports Festival in 1990, people were saying to me, "Aren't you happy you won?" I'd answer, "Yes, of course I am." Then they'd say, "Well, you don't *look* happy." That's when I realized what I had done to myself.

Now when I see young skaters in the locker room who are upset about a bad practice or competition but trying not to show it, I'll tell them, "Go ahead and get upset. Cry if you want to. Let your feelings out. Then go out there and try it again."

AT THE 1991 U.S. Championships in Minneapolis, Minnesota, most of the media and public attention focused on skaters Kristi Yamaguchi and Tonya Harding, who were expected to finish in the top two places. I was happy to let everyone focus on them, leaving me to concentrate only on skating to the best of my ability. In the end, the predictions came true. Tonya won the U.S. title, Kristi was second, and I was third, earning my first U.S. Championships medal.

Two moments stand out in my memories of Minneapolis. First, I received a very positive response from the audience when I introduced an element called an extended spiral at the end of my free program. This element is performed by gliding on one skate with my upper body parallel to the ice and my free leg lifted up behind me. The spiral combines body control and balance over the entire center of the ice, and I liked the way it fit into the overall program. I continued to include variations on this spiral in my programs after that.

I was even happier with how I overcame two mistakes at the beginning of that free program—mistakes that might have shattered my confidence in the past. In the first twenty seconds, I tried a double Axel jump and fell. This stunned me. I'd been landing double Axels since I was a novice and considered them fairly easy. This mistake had me so rattled that I made another just fifteen seconds later, on my next jump. It wasn't as bad as a fall, but instead of spinning three times for a triple flip jump, I only managed two spins before the landing.

At this point, I had a choice. I could let "the voice" tell me I was in big trouble and start worrying about how many more mistakes I would make during the next four minutes, or I could put my stress training into action and fight back by taking a deep breath to relax. In the middle of a performance, you have only a split second for this type of decision. Somehow, I managed to block out the two errors and went on to finish my program without another problem.

I won the bronze medal and received high marks from the nine judges. Most of my scores ranged between 5.6 and 5.8 on a point scale that goes up to 6.0. Even one more small mistake and I probably would have finished fourth like the year before. Instead, I had qualified to represent the U.S. at the World Championships along with Kristi and Tonya.

There was only one month between the end of our national competition and the start of "Worlds," which Munich,

Germany, hosted. Before I arrived with Mary and Evy, I'd decided not to worry about my scores or where I would place. I was about to compete in my first World Championships. The world's best skaters would be there—and I was one of them!

I didn't think I had much chance to win a medal, so my coaches and I didn't talk about it. But I was confident that I could skate clean programs and leave Munich feeling pleased about finishing the season on a positive note. Doing that, I told myself, would be a personal victory.

After the short program, I was fourth behind Kristi, Tonya, and Midori Ito of Japan, who was the 1989 world champion. There was one day off until the free program event and, as in Minneapolis, reporters were busy writing about the big showdown for the gold medal. Although Kristi was in first place after the short program, the long program counted for 66.7 percent of the total score, so there was no guarantee that she would win. Since I was in fourth place, I was still just on the outside of the spotlight, and I kept reminding myself that I had not expected to be in the middle of it.

When the deciding afternoon finally arrived, I felt as relaxed as possible, considering the crowd and TV cameras waiting to watch my every move. I focused all my concentration on the only thing I could control—my performance. In some ways, what happened to me was similar to what happened in Minneapolis the month before. I made a mistake—falling at the end of a triple salchow jump—but this time it came near the end of a solid program. Earlier, I had even completed two consecutive triple jumps during a part of the performance where I had practiced a double-triple combination. I left the ice feeling great.

As in many major competitions, one of the medal contenders ran into trouble. On that day it was Midori. She had suffered bruised ribs in a collision two days before and, still hurting, missed several jumps. When the judges' marks were counted, I placed third behind Kristi, the world champion, and Tonya, the silver medalist. I could hardly believe that I had won a medal—or, better yet, that I had become a part of skating history. Never before had three skaters from the same country finished in 1-2-3 order at a World Championships.

When we went to the center of the ice to receive our medals, there was a short delay because the event officials couldn't seem to find a third American flag. They probably didn't think they'd need three handy. But that crisis was soon resolved and as our national anthem was played to honor Kristi's victory, all three flags rose toward the ceiling.

The Munich World Championships were one of the most rewarding experiences of my skating career. Although I didn't realize it at the time, that competition would set off major changes in my life on and off the ice. After Munich, I realized for the first time that I might become an Olympian myself.

To qualify for the 1992 Winter Games I would need to place among the top three women at the U.S. Championships, which were now only ten months away. I felt more certain that I could earn one of those spots because not only had I just won two bronze medals, but I now knew that I could ignore my nerves and the voice inside my head and skate well in competition. This is a revelation every athlete wants to experience after years and years of hard work. It feels like being set free.

Chapter 4

B Y THE BEGINNING of the summer after the 1991
World Championships, the good feelings I'd had in
Munich were like a distant memory.

The reason was simple: My ankles hurt. This may
sound silly, but the pain was more than just the ache you have
when you've been too busy to sit down all day. I was suffer-
ing from tendinitis, which means the tendons across the
front of my ankles were inflamed and sore. This problem,
called "lace bite," is familiar to skaters. It's caused by the tight-
ness of the laces around my ankles, which put pressure against
my skin, almost as if the laces were cutting into the tendons.
The pain made it impossible for me to skate more than a few
minutes at a time. It even hurt when the tongue on my sneak-
ers touched the fronts of my ankles.

My doctors told me to stay off the ice until the inflam-
mation was gone and not just for a few days. They were thinking about six to eight weeks. To me, that might as well have
been six months. I couldn't imagine not skating for that
long, and it was scary to think about all the work I'd have to
do once I got back on the ice. Swimming was about the only

exercise I could do without irritating the tendons, so I practiced jumps in the water. This didn't help much, and I knew I had a lot of work ahead of me.

However, I soon decided that this was not a good time to start feeling sorry for myself. Everything I had ever accomplished as a skater was the result of overcoming obstacles, whether they were learning new jumps, adjusting to new coaches, or my own nerves. I was determined to keep going, if only because I wanted to experience again the feeling of soaring over the ice. So I put my skates aside and concentrated on swimming and weight training during the summer to stay in shape without causing more trouble for my feet.

It was the right decision. I felt so rejuvenated when I got back on the ice at the end of the summer that I welcomed the chance to train a little longer and work a little harder than normal. My coaches and I decided to keep the same programs I had performed in 1991, so I wasn't as worried about the lost training time. Skaters often carry programs from one season to the next, especially when they are comfortable with the music and choreography. Plus, I knew I could make my programs even better in 1992.

My confidence came right back and soon my jumps and spins did, too. I skated well in my fall competitions, especially at the Nations Cup event in Germany, where I finished first against skaters from all over the world. By January 1992, I had forgotten all about my sore feet and knew I was ready for the U.S. Championships in Orlando, Florida.

It was hard not to be excited about the next couple of months. For one thing, the United States's reputation in the world of figure skating had never been better. As top medalists in the previous year's World Championships, Kristi, Tonya, and I were serious contenders for Olympic medals as well. And we had some talented male skaters—Christopher Bowman, Todd Eldredge, and my friend Paul Wylie—who also were considered Olympic medal prospects. Todd recently had won a bronze in Munich; Christopher and Paul were 1988 Olympians. In pairs skating, Natasha Kuchiki and Todd Sand also had collected a bronze medal at the previous year's Worlds.

But before any of us could think about the upcoming Winter Olympics in France, we had to get through our national championships—which were far more important because it was an Olympic year. Under international rules, the U.S. was eligible to send three women and three men to the 1992 Olympics because we'd placed at least one skater in the top three of each division in Munich ten months earlier. If I placed fourth, it would not just be the disappointment of failing to win a medal that I'd have to live with. This time, it would mean the difference between skating in the Olympics or watching them on television.

When we finished the short program portion of the competition, it was immediately obvious that the experience of the prior season was paying off. At the senior level, the pressure of the short program event is intense. If you're not ranked in the top four or five after that event, your chance of moving up to the medal stand is bleak. A mistake or two can take you out of contention, so you can lose everything you've worked for in less than three minutes.

As most people had predicted, Kristi was in first place after the short program. I avoided any serious mistakes and was right behind her in second place. Tonya was third. I was relieved to be positioned comfortably in second place, but anxious to get on to Saturday's competition, when the Olympic team would be decided.

My free program, skated to music from *Born on the Fourth of July* and *Siesta* by Miles Davis, had the same look as the one I performed in 1991, but it was more challenging. I had added a triple jump and now would attempt a total of seven triples during the four and a half minutes. When I was learning the triples as a teenager, I don't think I ever imagined trying seven in one program, but women's skating had evolved rapidly in just a few short years. Suddenly, this was the magic number for anyone hoping for a medal in a major competition.

There are actually just six different jumps—Axel, flip, loop, lutz, toe loop, and salchow—and each can be performed as doubles (two spins) or triples (three spins). Rules allow for a maximum of two different jumps to be repeated in the same program, and even then the repeated jump must be done in combination with another jump.

Unless you have actually tried them, it is sometimes difficult to recognize the differences between jumps. The Axel is the easiest to recognize because it's the only jump that begins with a forward takeoff and has an extra half-spin in the air. For example, a triple Axel is actually three and a half spins rather than three. The other five jumps begin as the skater is moving backward. Basically, the six jumps are distinguished by whether a skater takes off with a toe-pick—the jagged "teeth" at the front of both blades—or with an "edge" of the blade. The toe-pick jumps are the lutz, flip, and toe loop. The edge jumps are the Axel, salchow, and loop.

Also, even if you see a skater land a jump without falling, the judges still might deduct from his score. Deductions are made in tenths of a point. A jump landed on two feet instead of one foot or one that ends with a skater putting a hand down on the ice to break a fall is not considered a clean jump.

For free programs, the rules don't require jumps to be

performed in a certain order and no rule says how many double or triple jumps you must try. The number and types of jumps necessary to contend for a medal is really decided by the skaters. In the late 1980s, top women's skaters started trying five and six triple jumps in their programs. As soon as a few were doing that many, it meant the younger skaters, including me, would one day also have to try five, six, and, eventually, seven.

That's also true of the types of jumps. When Midori Ito became the first woman to land a triple Axel in 1989, it was only a matter of time before others would try to match her. Tonya Harding's first triple Axel—and the first by a U.S. woman—came along in 1991 when she won the U.S. championship. Tonya landed another a month later when she finished second to Kristi in Munich.

The triple Axel was a major topic as we waited for the free program competition to begin at the 1992 Championships. Tonya had a proven ability to land a triple Axel in her program; Kristi and I did not. If each of us skated a clean program—no falls or stumbles—some people assumed the judges would give Tonya the highest marks because the triple Axel is by far the most challenging jump of the six. At this point, both Kristi and I had worked on triple Axels but still couldn't land them often enough. It was too risky to put a jump in your program that wasn't ready yet. If you try it and fall, not only will the judges mark you down but the disappointment—not to mention the pain—of crashing on the ice can destroy your confidence and cause mistakes in the remainder of the program. That's when "the voice" can really start shouting in your ears.

My coaches and I believed it was far more important to deliver a great program, one that showcased both athleticism and artistry, than to worry about the effect of one jump by another skater. Kristi and her coach felt the same way. In a competition with as much tension as the U.S. Championships, it just doesn't make sense to assume anything, especially that all of the "favorites" will skate clean programs. You can only control your own skating. What other skaters do or fail to do is out of your hands.

I was fortunate to believe that when I went out to skate for a place on the U.S. Olympic team in Orlando. My performance was not perfect, yet I made it through without a serious fall or break in concentration, landing four of the seven triple jumps. The other three became doubles instead of triples. Sometimes, it's wiser to land a clean double than to force yourself to do a triple, especially when you know from years of experience that you have too little momentum on the takeoff to complete the third spin.

I was most proud of the fact that I was able to adjust to one little mistake by adding a jump later in the program. In the first minute, I was planning to try a triple-triple combination jump—two triple toe loop jumps in a row. This is the combination that I first had mastered when I was just fifteen, seven years earlier. But in Orlando, I only managed to land the first triple toe. I knew when I landed it that going back up for the second triple toe would be a bad idea.

So I went on with the program, all the while keeping in the back of my mind that I could try another triple toe loop later on. When you create a program, you always leave a couple of little openings, just in case you need to add a jump. With about thirty seconds remaining, I saw my chance and set myself up for a triple toe–double toe combination jump. In just a few seconds, it was over. I landed both jumps, finished with my extended spiral, and left the ice knowing I'd done close to my best.

Kristi, meanwhile, won her first U.S. championship in singles with a nearly perfect program in which she landed all of her seven planned triple jumps. Tonya finished third. She fell at the end of a triple Axel and was bothered throughout her performance by pain from a pulled muscle in her right ankle.

Both Kristi and Tonya had skated before me, but I didn't watch them—this is a personal rule of mine and one that's shared by most other skaters—and I had no idea how their marks compared to mine. But after my marks were posted and automatically calculated into the overall standings, I finished second, won the silver medal, and earned a chance to do it all over again at the Winter Olympics in a French town called Albertville.

AFTER WE ARRIVED in France, we settled into our housing at the athletes' village, about thirty minutes by bus from the skating arena. We stayed two to a room because space in the village was limited, but I was pleased by this arrangement because Kristi was my roommate. Skating in so many of the same events over the past seven years had given us a chance to become friends even though our homes were so far apart. Kristi, who is two years younger than me, is from northern California and had done most of her recent training with a coach who lived in Edmonton, Canada. With about two weeks ahead of us in France, we agreed to have as much fun as possible at these Olympics and try to keep each other from becoming too scared or nervous as the competition drew closer.

Unfortunately, the first three days of my Olympic experience didn't go as planned. I had bronchitis for a week before I left home and my coaches decided that I had to take it easy. This kept me off the ice but my coaches told me not worry about the missed practice time since they thought I probably needed a little break. It wasn't long before I started feeling better and found out they were right. When I finally started practicing my programs again, I was more excited than worried about getting ready. My main task was to get comfortable with the ice and the inside of the Olympic ice arena.

One of the best decisions I made was to try to get out now and then to see what else was going on at the Games. Unlike all of the other skating competitions, where you mostly practice, rest at the hotel, and concentrate on your programs, the Olympics offer all kinds of wonderful diversions. Paul Wylie, who was training in the same rink with me in Massachusetts, also had qualified for the team and it was great to be able to rely on our friendship during the time we spent in France.

I don't think I've ever had as much fun as I had at the Olympic Games in Albertville. I'd get together with a bunch of other athletes to eat in the cafeteria or, if I went by myself, I'd just go up to anyone wearing a USA jacket and ask if I could join them. We'd go shopping in the Olympic village or someone would bring a radio into one of the dorm rooms and we'd listen to music and talk. I got to know some of the ski jumpers, and one day after the skating competition was over, we all went downhill skiing. We'd hit the bumps on the trail and jump off them. They were surprised that I could match their pace down the mountain!

The men's competition was scheduled in the first week, which gave the women's team a chance to feel the tension inside the arena before it was our turn. Paul was definitely an inspiration. He skated one of the best free programs of his career—not one mistake—to move up from third place after the short program and win the silver medal.

As I watched the men receive their medals, I was thinking how much I would enjoy having the same experience. And it wasn't long before that chance would be at my fingertips. Over the next few days, my parents, brothers, and other family members arrived in France. It was great having us all in one place again, but I was starting to feel a little more uptight as February 19 arrived. CBS set up a special TV monitor for my mom by the ice so that she could watch me—and CBS could watch both of us.

Fortunately, I put on a solid performance in the short program for my mom and everyone else and wound up in second place, right behind Kristi, who was skating just as well as she had in Orlando. The French skater Surya Bonaly was third and Midori Ito was fourth. Our teammate Tonya Harding took a fall after a triple jump and was marked down to sixth place.

Suddenly, the 1992 Olympics had come down to one final night. At this point, I knew I could do my program in my sleep. I was pleased with how my practice sessions had been going. I had seen Paul Wylie's wonderful performance with my own eyes the week before. But I found it almost impossible to force myself to be calm. Apparently, I was not the only one who felt this way.

The six top-ranked skaters after the short program are the last group to perform in the long program. By the luck of the draw, Kristi was the first to skate in the last group. I followed her. The battle for the medals came down to a contest of who could make the fewest mistakes on a night when almost everyone seemed to slip and stumble—everyone but Kristi. She did have one fall on a triple jump, but the rest of her program was skated like a true champion. The arena held about nine thousand spectators, including several thousand Americans waving flags and banners. After Kristi's performance, the crowd was pretty pumped up. Then it was my turn.

Wearing a white dress with a diamond-studded neckline designed by Vera Wang, I went to the center of the ice to await the now-familiar music from *Born on the Fourth of July* and began skating a program that had been a part of my life for the past eighteen months. Right away, I understood why the Olympics are known as such a severe test of skill and composure. I felt a little ripple of panic run through my body and shortly after that, I set up for a triple-double jump combination. Landing the second jump, I came down with too much forward momentum. I had to make a choice—fall or stick out a hand to get my balance. Instinctively, my hand shot out and I was still standing. But the judges now had to deduct at least two-tenths of a point from my score. Whatever confidence I had left felt as if it drained out of me. Later in my program, I took off for a triple jump and there was nothing there. My legs felt frozen. I only managed a single spin. The same thing happened again near the end.

Leaving the ice after my performance, I knew the last four and a half minutes had not been the best of my career. But the great feeling of relief, maybe even of survival, and the applause and cheering from the crowd snapped me back to reality. I hadn't fallen down or fallen apart. I hadn't given up. My scores —ranging between 5.6 and 5.8—were certainly not embarrassing. There was nothing more I could do but watch and wait.

Those who skated after me also struggled, although Midori Ito managed to land the first triple Axel in the history of Olympic women's skating and finished her program with a powerful display of jumps and spins. Twenty minutes later, the marks were in. Now, all eyes were on computer monitors placed throughout the arena. My mom and dad had decided I would probably finish fourth, but were hoping they were wrong.

The digital scoreboards went blank for a split second and then I heard the crowd roar. As expected, Kristi was the gold medalist. Midori had finished second. And, next to the number "3," it read: NANCY KERRIGAN, USA.

Back home in Stoneham, there are dozens of medals with my name on them. Now there would be another—the bronze medal from the 1992 Olympic Winter Games. I went back to Massachusetts a few days later. There was a parade through the streets of Stoneham and a banner with my name on it placed across the front of the town hall. A little street next to the Stoneham Arena was renamed Nancy Kerrigan Way. I enjoyed every moment, but the celebration was short. I was still training every day for the 1992 World Championships in Oakland, California, where I won a silver medal only a month after the Olympics.

Kristi had gone on to win her second world title in Oakland, practically down the street from where she grew up. A couple of weeks later, Kristi announced her retirement from amateur skating, saying that she planned to continue appearing in professional shows and tours. I knew it would seem strange no longer having her around, but stranger still was the idea that I would be expected to win the 1993 U.S. title the following February in Phoenix, Arizona.

Chapter 5

I TURNED TWENTY-THREE a few months before we arrived in Phoenix for the 1993 U.S. Championships. Until then, I'd never thought about being the "old woman" of the senior division. But in Phoenix I was the only senior female in the singles competition born in the 1960s—October 13, 1969, to be exact.

Still, it wasn't long before I was reminded that age equals experience, and that experience is hard to beat. A new free program, choreographed to music from *Beauty and the Beast*, had come together well during the summer, even though I was busier than ever, balancing practices and workouts with some new responsibilities. My success in 1992 created several opportunities to work with large corporations who paid me to make appearances and share my stories from the previous season, especially the Olympics.

In many ways, what happened in Phoenix was not unlike the story of the Winter Olympics. On the day of the free program competition, almost all of the contenders found themselves making mistakes and falling. In France the previous winter, Kristi Yamaguchi had been the one to make only

41

minor mistakes and come out on top. This time, it was me. I fell trying a triple lutz jump early in the program and generally felt I was rushing into everything. But since I was in first place after the short program, the marks I received for the free program were high enough to keep me ahead of the others. Eighteen years after my first skating lesson, I was the national champion.

Afterward, I told reporters I was saving room to improve for the World Championships, coming up a month later. I really felt that way and went right back to work when I returned home. So many positive things had happened in the past year, I guess I never stopped to take a close look at where it was all heading. But it finally hit me like a strong gust of wind when I traveled to the 1993 Worlds hosted by Prague in the Czech Republic.

By now, Kristi and Midori Ito were gone. Tonya Harding had been fourth in Phoenix and had not qualified for the U.S. World Championships team. There was a young new generation of talented skaters coming up, but many were still unproven in major competition. Under these circumstances, I was not just the new U.S. champion. Some people saw me as the most likely winner of the world title in Prague. And that wasn't all. I also was considered a favorite to become the next Olympic champion.

A few years earlier, the International Olympic Committee had voted to separate the Winter and Summer Olympics. Since 1924, they had held both events about six months apart every four years. The only way to change this pattern was to add an extra Winter Olympics. This meant there would be a Winter Olympics in 1994, a Summer Olympics in 1996, another Winter Olympics in 1998, and so on. So at the time of the 1993 World Figure Skating Championships, the next

Winter Olympics were less than one year away.

When it came to skating, I thought I was mature enough by now to go into the rink, identify problems with my performances, and work on making them better. But I had no experience with handling the enormous weight of rising to number one in the world. The closest I had come was standing next to Kristi on the medals platform, looking up and being proud of her. Since childhood, my love of skating always had been my motivation for going on. I rarely thought about being a world champion, and I certainly never talked about it with my parents or with Mary and Evy.

I guess I went to Prague trying to pretend that the challenge of skating for the world gold medal was no big deal. Strangely enough, nothing happened in the short program competition to convince me otherwise. This was the same short program that had carried me to Olympic bronze and World silver medals the year before. And I skated every bit as well, landing a combination triple lutz–double toe loop jump at the start and going on from there without error. Six of the nine judges gave me first place marks and I was the leader going into the free program two days later.

As always, the last phase of the event counted 66.7 percent toward the final placement, so there was no guarantee I had secured the gold medal. However, I'd also been skating very well in the practices, hitting every jump and spin consistently, so I was feeling confident.

On the night of the final competition, I went on the ice for the usual six-minute warm-up, then skated off and waited for my turn to perform. I was the last to skate, so I had forty-five minutes to wait. I just sat backstage for that entire time, getting more and more nervous. "The voice" started whispering in my head: *I've been skating so well. I have to do this. I have to. I have to. I have to . . .*

I finally skated onto the ice to compete, but by this time I had put so much pressure on myself that I felt stiff all over. I wasn't even bending my knees, and you *have* to bend your knees in order to jump in the air! The entire performance was like a bad dream. I would set up for jumps, feel fine, and miss them anyway. Three times, I launched into the air expecting a triple jump, and three times I landed without one, settling for singles or doubles instead.

I was totally stunned as I came off the ice. I even looked at Mary and asked her if I could go out to skate my program again. The hours after I skated were worse than the four and a half minutes in front of the judges. I ran the ordeal through my mind again and again and still couldn't understand how I'd let myself fall apart like that. Taking the words from the title of my long program music, a newspaper reported on my awful performance the next day by saying that the beauty had taken on the beast, and the beast won.

Not only did I fail to win the gold, I also managed to take myself out of contention for the silver and the bronze as well. I was rated only ninth best on the final day and ended up placing fifth overall. For the first time in more than two and a half years, I would be leaving a skating competition without a medal of any color. The new world champion was not Nancy Kerrigan but a fifteen-year-old from the Ukraine named Oksana Baiul.

I wasn't happy about it at the time, but in many ways this was a good test of my will and determination as both an athlete and a person. I'd never believed in quitting, not as a little kid trying to play hockey with my big brothers and not when I was learning to master triple jumps by spending a fair amount of time landing on my backside. If ever there was a

time to seriously ask the question—"Do I want to quit?"—
that time had come. But I knew I couldn't leave the sport on
this negative note—and that I'd be unhappy if I didn't give
myself a chance to make another Olympic team the following year. And I couldn't erase the one question that kept pop-
ping into my mind: "What if your best days in skating are
still to come?" It would have been a shame to always have to
live with that question, so I committed myself to finding the
answer.

Back home, I quickly realized that not all of the solutions
to my many problems in Prague would be worked out on the
ice. The game plan had to go beyond the boundaries of our
skating rink in Cape Cod.

First, I decided that some of the extra activities and spe
cial appearances had to go. I could no longer just hop on air-
planes and take off for days at a time.

Second, I bought an exercise videotape called *Abs of Steel*,
which showed how to strengthen stomach and back muscles
and put together a harder exercise schedule to improve my
endurance.

Finally, I called on Cindy Adams, a sports psychologist and
former skater. In the spring of 1993, I began meeting with
Cindy about once a week. I talked, she listened. Eventually,
she put her finger on one of the ways I could improve my men-
tal preparations in the weeks or months leading to a competition.

"Practice competing," she said. From what I was describ-
ing, Cindy believed I was changing my routine too much from
day to day. She suggested I go into the rink as if I was enter-
ing an arena to skate a short or long program, sort of like doing
a dress rehearsal. The theory was that I would be much more
comfortable right before an actual performance if I felt

like I was back home in my regular rink.

We also figured out what I should do during the time I had to wait before competing. Sitting still for forty-five minutes before skating at Prague hadn't been a good idea—but I had no idea what else to do. Sometimes I'd put on my costume while I was waiting, sometimes I wouldn't. Sometimes I'd try to stretch, sometimes I wouldn't. I never knew if I had enough time to take my skates off. And sometimes I sat still because I thought that if I used up too much energy, I wouldn't have any left when it came time to skate—which was rather ridiculous, since I trained by skating for four hours *every day.*

A lot of skaters have the same problem with waiting. Some won't take off their skates, even if they're not going to perform for an hour, because they're afraid they'll relace their boots incorrectly. Again, this isn't logical—skaters relace their boots many times a day when they're training. But when your nerves kick in, you start worrying about the strangest things, things that don't bother you on a daily basis.

Together, Cindy and I came up with routines that I would use while waiting. I had several different routines depending on whether my wait was two minutes, twenty minutes, a half an hour, or forty-five minutes. During practice, I'd rehearse these routines. I'd warm up for six minutes, then come off the ice and say, "OK, I've got a forty-five-minute wait. I'm going to take off my skates and sprint up and down the hallways for a certain number of times. Then I'm going to do my stretches. Then I'll put my skates back on . . ." and so on. It took some time to figure all this out, but when we were done, I was confident that I knew exactly how to handle my time off the ice, as well as on.

Going into the 1993–94 skating season, Prague seemed as though it had never happened. I was more prepared than ever before in my career. And, thanks to a lot of hard work and sweat, I was in great physical shape, lighter but stronger. More often than not, I was going to the rink, turning on my music, skating through my program with clean, powerful jumps, and then doing it all over again. I'd just rewind the tape and go.

The first evidence that my new approach to training would be rewarded came along in October 1993 when we flew to Norway for a competition called Piruetten. This was an unusually important event for two reasons. Top skaters from around the world were coming in to try out new programs, including Chen Lu of China and Surya Bonaly, prospective Olympic medal contenders. And we would be skating in the arena built for the 1994 Winter Games in the Norwegian town of Hamar. It was a sneak preview of the Olympics, you might say, with just three months to go.

In Hamar, I unveiled two brand-new programs—a short program to another selection by Mark Militano, *Desperate Love*, and a long program set to a medley of Neil Diamond music performed by the Boston Pops orchestra.

Considering it was still early in the season, I could not have been happier about the outcome. I skated both programs with only very minor errors and never felt the slightest doubt that I was capable of winning. And I did win. My long program was especially reassuring because I landed six triple jumps and felt just as strong at the end as I had at the beginning.

About six weeks later, I skated in a new type of competition called a Pro-Am, in which skaters are awarded prize money. In the women's event, I was one of three amateur skaters—those eligible for the U.S. Championships and Olympics as registered members of the USFSA—competing in a field with two professional skaters.

(Although amateurs are allowed to earn money through skating, the money must be earned in events run by the USFSA or the International Skating Union, the organizations that set the rules of amateur skating. Skaters are considered professionals when they choose to earn money in competitions that are not approved by the USFSA and ISU. This decision makes them ineligible for the U.S. Championships, Olympics, and World Championships.)

My performances at the Pro-Am were as strong as they had been in Norway. I placed first in both the short and long programs, which earned me a prize of $40,000. After my family had spent thousands of dollars for so many years to allow me to develop as a skater, it was nice to have this reward. But I was even more pleased by how well I was skating and by how I was able to compete as well as I practiced. I felt that I was really in control.

During the Pro-Am, I was interviewed by reporters from some of the country's biggest newspapers. Everyone wanted to know if I considered myself a favorite to win my second gold medal at the U.S. Championships, which were now less than one month away. In the past I might not have wanted to answer that question. It can be dangerous to make predictions because you might end up placing too much pressure on yourself. But I couldn't deny what I really felt, so I answered with the truth: "Yes, I am the favorite."

My confidence was soaring primarily because my attitude was so positive. The big change had come about back in October, even before we went over to the Piruetten event in

Norway. One afternoon, to the utter amazement of Evy, I walked into the rink in Cape Cod, put on my skates, and went out and did a full run-through of my long program as if it was being judged. I made no mistakes and never paused in the middle, as I had so often in the past. Evy had never seen me do that in the more than seven years we had worked together.

The way I used to train—and the way the other skaters I knew trained—was to start skating a program and, if you fall on the first jump, you stop the music, rewind the tape, and start again. If you then fall on the second jump, you start all over again. You don't go to the end of the program until you hit every jump and spin.

It's hard not to practice this way because it's so frustrating when you fall on a jump. Of course, you want to try it again. But if you fall in a competition, you can't say, "Excuse me, I want to start over." They just won't let you do it!

So I had to change my routine and skate in my practices as if they were competitions. If I fell, I had to learn to forget about that mistake and keep going. I also learned to take each element one at a time. If I'm in a spin and I'm thinking of the next jump, then my spin's probably off balance and I'll lose speed. So I learned to focus: OK, now I'm in the spin, now I'm going into the jump, and so on. One thing at a time.

Eventually, I could perform my long program two times in a row without so much as a stumble. That was important because, if you can make it through your program twice in a row and skate for eight minutes without dying at the end, then you can manage one time through in competition with the lights and the nerves and the judges and the crowd.

Right before we flew to Philadelphia, Pennsylvania, Evy and I were chatting about all of the progress I'd made since

49

the last World Championships. He finally asked me a question I think had been on his mind for quite some time. He wanted to know why I had not trained like this in previous years and why I never made a habit of skating programs from beginning to end without stopping.

I told him that there were a number of reasons I had started training more intensely. Cindy Adams had suggested it, for one. And I was in much better physical shape than ever before. But the real difference was that I'd always hesitated to attempt a perfect program at the training rink because I was afraid to find out that I couldn't do one. Now the fear was gone, and with the 1994 U.S. Championships coming up in just a few weeks, I was convinced I would skate well enough to win another title, make it onto my second Olympic team and, if I was really fortunate, even win the Olympic gold medal in February. The first stop on the journey would be Detroit, Michigan, and I couldn't wait to get started.

The scenario in Detroit wasn't very different from what it had been at the previous Championships eleven months earlier in Phoenix. Tonya Harding and I were the two most experienced skaters in the women's senior division. We'd both won a national championship and skated under pressure in major competitions. I think most people agreed that we were both likely to qualify for the 1994 Olympic team, assuming we avoided injury and managed to land the triple jumps when it counted.

According to most newspaper reports, Tonya and I were rivals. I wasn't sure what that meant because I certainly had not gone to Detroit to win a contest against Tonya Harding. Few, if any, skaters focus their training on defeating another skater. The sport just doesn't work that way. It is not like two sprinters side by side in a race, trying to reach the finish line first. As a result, skaters get along well. We're not always best friends but we tend to be friendly, and we certainly understand better than anyone else what it feels like to stand alone in the middle of the ice, waiting to start a performance.

Tonya and I had skated in the same events for the past six or seven years, and we had traveled in some of the ice shows that tour the U.S. in the spring and early summer. We were even roommates for about a week in the fall of 1987 at the NHK Trophy competition in Japan. But even then I rarely saw her and had the impression that she didn't want to be a part of "the group." In the years that followed, we always exchanged hellos, but there was almost never any small talk. Most of what I knew about her I read in the newspapers just like everybody else.

As always, when we first saw each other in Detroit, coming or going from the practice ice, we'd said "hi" and "good luck" and that was about it.

When I awoke on the morning of January 6, 1994, in my Detroit hotel room, the competition for senior women was still about thirty-six hours away. The biggest news to that point had been all the snow that was building up on the downtown streets and sidewalks. But the skaters were paying little attention to the weather. We were thinking only about what was going on indoors.

At most competitions, skaters and coaches are given a practice schedule. Each skater is assigned to a practice group, which is identified by a letter, usually A, B, and C. Because there are so many skaters in the National Championships, ice time must be tightly controlled so everyone has a chance to train. This schedule plans your day for you, so it's the one piece of paper you carry around and try not to lose.

My group was assigned to practice that afternoon, starting at 1:30, on an ice surface put down especially for the Championships. This practice rink was in an enormous convention hall, right next door to Joe Louis Arena in downtown Detroit. As we went through our programs, one skater at a time, a big international car show was going on upstairs in the hall and the pairs skaters were competing over in the arena.

Our session ended after an hour. Just a few minutes past 2:30, I left the ice, slid blade covers over my skating blades, and walked to the dressing room to change clothes. This was something I have done hundreds of times in dozens of different cities.

My practice had gone well. I felt confident and ready to face the judges. I was a little concerned about soreness on the side of my calf caused by a pulled muscle, and I'd talked to someone about seeing a physical therapist later that day. Otherwise, I felt great.

Then I saw a flash in the corner of my eye. Someone seemed to come from behind me on my right. I turned around just in time to see an arm and what looked like a stick moving in a downward motion. Then I felt it. My right leg was throbbing. I tried to take a couple of steps but the pain was indescribable, and I quickly realized it was silly to try walking. I sat down on the cement floor and screamed.

Suddenly, the world of skating as I knew it had changed. It seemed that everything was beyond my control. Someone had attacked me and run away. And now I found myself in a hospital, where doctors were examining my right leg and taking a series of X rays, hoping for a clearer picture of how much damage had been done.

All I knew for sure was that my leg hurt and was becoming more swollen by the minute. Soon, I couldn't move it very much. I couldn't even walk. There was no way I was going to skate in Detroit the next day, even though I kept insisting that I would be OK by then. My attempts to take even a few steps had failed but I remember pleading with the doctors: "Just let me try it again. I can do it!"

Late that night we held a press conference to announce that I was out of the competition. I forced myself to appear calm, though I was not. I didn't want everyone to see how upset I was. I wanted to be strong. But I was still going through different stages of emotion. Part of it was sadness, the other part was anger. It wasn't that I was scared of being attacked again, or paranoid. I couldn't get it out of my mind how unbelievable it all seemed. It was total shock.

I stayed in Detroit for the rest of the week because everyone thought it would be best if I was treated there. The U.S. skating team doctor, Mahlon Bradley, worked closely with the local doctors, and my physical therapist had flown in the day of the attack. Over the next few days, I found that the best thing for me to do was try and think about the future and about getting my leg back in shape. The doctors said my X rays were clean—no broken bones. Luckily, the person who attacked me missed my kneecap. If his aim had been better, I might have been through with skating forever. I might have needed major surgery just to be able to walk again.

So even though there was a little good news, those three nights in Detroit were not easy. I had trouble sleeping and when I did manage to fall asleep, I was dreaming about my knee. I don't remember the dreams with much detail, but there were several times when I'd wake up and grab my right leg. Unfortunately, that made my leg start throbbing all over again.

As doctors examined my knee each day, they agreed that

the swelling would probably be temporary and that it could heal in a matter of weeks. But I had a lot of work to do. The Winter Olympics in Norway were just six weeks away. After the USFSA agreed to name me to the Olympic team—as long as I could prove myself ready to skate—I went home to Massachusetts.

Chapter 6

J UST TWELVE DAYS after the attack in Detroit, I was back
on the ice at the Stoneham Arena. By now, three men were
under arrest in Portland, Oregon—Tonya Harding's
hometown—and charged by police with carrying out a
plot to injure me. Among the three were Shawn Eckhardt,
who claimed to work for Tonya as a bodyguard, and Shane
Stant, accused of following me to Detroit and striking my leg
with a metal club. He was to be paid several thousand dollars for completing the assignment. Jeff Gillooly, Tonya's former husband, was arrested a few days after the others turned
themselves in to police.

This was the number one news story in the United States
in the early weeks of 1994. Every newspaper and dozens of
television shows were covering it. TV camera crews and clus-
ters of photographers camped out on the street in front of
my family's house from morning to night.

Three thousand miles away, cameras filmed Tonya's practices in Portland. She, too, was getting ready for the Olympics,
having won the U.S. championship in Detroit. It was impossible for her to train in privacy because her rink was located
inside a shopping mall. Some people believed that Tonya knew

about the plan, but she denied it, saying she only found out what the other four were up to after I was attacked.

Meanwhile, I was spending my days out of sight inside the Lexington Club, a fitness center with an indoor swimming pool. By now, I was working with a rehabilitation team that included Dr. Mahlon Bradley, who monitored the flexibility of my right knee, my therapist Vinny Buscemi, and Igor Burdenko, a trainer who also does massage therapy.

We had one goal: restore the strength of my leg as quickly as possible so I could return to the ice and practice my Olympic programs as if nothing had happened. I was totally committed to that goal, but therapy is no fun. Some of the exercises were painful because my knee was still "remembering" how to bend. Plus, it takes days and days of work to see only minor progress. But I never felt as if I had a choice. The work had to be done, and I was determined to show the people who attacked me that I would not allow them to keep me out of the Olympics.

My days were divided into segments. In the pool, I went through a series of water exercises. These allowed me to improve my knee's flexibility without the jarring impact of a gym floor or an ice surface; it was also a good overall program for keeping the rest of my body fit.

Next I worked in the weight room with Vinny. We used pulley ropes with weights attached to my leg to put pressure on the knee. When I pulled down on the rope, my knee would move backward. Each day, it would bend a little more as the muscles became more conditioned. I'd also place weights under my feet and march in place. I did three sets of thirty steps each. To improve my balance, I practiced stepping up onto a weight-lifting bench one leg at a time, holding the position, and stepping back down. I really had to push myself to get through these repetitions, both because they were painful and because they were boring.

On the basketball court, I practiced the footwork and turns I do on the ice when I'm wearing skates. Except this was a little different. We would take about twenty feet of rubber surgical tubing, tying one end around my waist, the other end around a pole. The tubing provided resistance and helped me relearn the muscle control needed for landing a jump.

The worst part of the process was Igor's massage. It sounds great, of course: a leg massage every day. But his were extremely deep and intense, usually lasting ten to twenty minutes. It hurt so much my eyes would fill with tears. I was always happy when those sessions were over.

This was an incredibly intense period. My therapy took eight or nine hours a day, every day—no weekends off! I was working out in the glare of the media, which magnified everything that happened. And always, in the back of my mind, was the knowledge that I was getting ready for the Olympics, the biggest amateur sporting event in the world. I've never worked that hard in my life. I hope I never have to work that hard again!

Finally, the day approached when I was going to get on the ice again in front of my family, my coaches, and the press. This would be the deciding moment. Did all the work pay off? Was I going to be able to compete at the Olympics?

I was so anxious to skate again, but I didn't want to try it—for the first time since the attack—in front of the press. So the night before my official "return," I snuck into the ice rink after midnight, once the reporters had left from in front of our house. My parents and my brother Michael came with me; Michael resurfaced the ice for me. Dr. Bradley and Vinny also came along just in case anything went wrong. I skated around a little, just enough to know that I'd be fine the next morning.

Then, at 8:00 A.M. on January 17, I stepped onto the ice at my hometown rink. It felt as if I had been waiting for this day to come for a long time, but it had been less than two weeks since the attack. A CBS camera crew was there, along with six or seven newspaper and magazine reporters who had flown in the night before. Photographers were assembled everywhere as well. Mary and Evy took their usual viewing positions next to the ice against the barrier used for hockey games.

The drama ended quickly. It was obvious right away that I had not forgotten how to skate and, although my right knee was a little stiff, it seemed ready to cooperate. After a few minutes I was moving over the ice without many limitations, although I had been given strict orders not to try any jumps or spins until I had enough strength.

Practicing some footwork a few minutes later, I stumbled, lost my balance, and fell flat. You could almost hear everyone holding their breath. I realized immediately that I was unharmed and popped right back up, laughing. I never thought I would be so happy about falling down in front of the press. But it was impossible *not* to be happy—I knew my comeback was on schedule.

After a few more days, the doctors were not around the rink quite as often to watch my practices and I decided to start putting my leg to a real test. I was most anxious to try a sit-spin, an element you often see near the end of a skater's program. To do this spin, you bend the skating leg at the knee and drop into a crouch position. I found I could do one with my right leg bent without feeling much pain at all. (I couldn't crouch into this position while standing still but, because of the force of spinning, it was—strangely enough—easier to drop into this position in a spin.) I continued to add more of the elements of my programs, all the while acting innocent when I'd meet with the doctors. I would ask, "When can I try a sit-spin?" And they'd say, "Not yet." So I would smile and reply, "Well, too late. I did one yesterday." Within another week I was rehearsing full run-throughs of my programs, landing all of the jumps as doubles and rarely thinking about my knee.

It's hard to explain what it was like when I was recovering from the attack, a period which really lasted until the day I competed. My energy and thoughts were so focused on what I had to do that it was like I was . . . somewhere else. I was "in the zone," that place of total concentration that athletes sometimes reach where every breath is devoted to achieving their goal.

I had so much to do that I didn't have time to eat. My coaches and family would say, "This is crazy; you have to eat or you'll have no energy." I knew they were right. I was losing so much weight that I began applying my blush backward to hide my sunken cheeks. I knew this wasn't healthy, but I was either too busy to eat or I'd feel full after taking only a few bites. Plus, I was using so much energy from training and nerves that any calories I did eat were quickly burned away. Soon, I realized that this could catch up with me and drain my energy. I forced myself to eat more and to get back to more healthy eating habits.

By now, I was used to training by running through my long program two times in a row without stopping. So I started running through my program *three* times in a row because I was so determined—almost obsessed—with skating well at the Olympics. Now the voice inside my head was saying: *I'm going to do it. I'm going to do it.* My pride kept me going. I didn't want to get to the Olympics and say, "Well, they let me compete because they knew I should be allowed to and I did a good job—but not what I could have done if I hadn't been hurt."

Before the Olympics, I even performed in an exhibition called "Nancy Kerrigan and Friends" to raise money for a charity called SightFirst, which aids research into the prevention and treatment of blindness. That was an important step for me because I was on the ice again—this time in front of a crowd. There would have been too much pressure if the first time I was in front of a crowd again had been at the Olympics!

Thanks to that rigorous physical therapy program, I was in better shape than ever before. Being in shape helps you practice more effectively and it gives you unbelievable confidence. I kept thinking how great it would be if the Olympics would start right away, so I could go out and show the world what Mary and Evy were seeing in the practice rink. As I had realized so many times in the past, you always get rewarded when you refuse to give up.

UNFORTUNATELY, public attention on the attack against me in Detroit was building rather than disappearing. At the beginning of February, about three weeks before Olympic women's skating was to begin on February 23, a USFSA review panel met to discuss all of the information that had been collected about the attack, including FBI reports. The panel decided that Tonya Harding did know about the plan carried out by her former husband, Jeff, and the other three men.

At this point, the United States Olympic Committee had to turn in a list of the U.S. team members who would be sent to Norway to represent our country. However, law enforcement officials in Oregon had not filed criminal charges against Tonya, so she wasn't under arrest. Even though the USFSA believed Tonya had something to do with the attack, it couldn't stop her from being a member of the Olympic team.

When I arrived in Norway about a week later, hundreds of reporters were waiting for me. Everyone was talking about Tonya, wondering if she would be making the trip. A few days later, the mystery ended. Tonya arrived and the Olympic Committee announced it would conduct a hearing of its own to decide if she would be allowed to skate. Meanwhile, the USFSA flew thirteen-year-old Michelle Kwan, the Olympic team alternate, to Norway just in case Tonya would be barred from competing. As it turned out, Michelle could have stayed home. Tonya's lawyers threatened to sue the Olympic Committee for twenty five million dollars, claiming that any steps to remove her from the team would be the same as announcing she was guilty of involvement in the plot. The Olympic Committee postponed the hearing. The U.S.'s 1994 Olympians in women's skating would be Nancy Kerrigan and Tonya Harding.

Although I continued practicing and undergoing therapy, working out daily in Norway with a stationary bicycle and a weight machine, I couldn't ignore what was happening around me. So much evidence connected Tonya to the plot, yet no one seemed able to do anything about it. At first, I tried to believe that she knew nothing about the attack. But that was before our talk a few weeks earlier with FBI officials, who already had spent close to ten hours interviewing Tonya. Not one person working on the case believed she was innocent. Not one. These investigators deal with these kinds of cases every day. They would not give Tonya the benefit of the doubt, and I decided it didn't make sense to give her that benefit in my own mind.

I was angry at the whole situation. It threw my life into turmoil—and yet we were involved in sports, not life-or-death situations. I also felt angry at the inability of Olympic officials to keep Tonya off the team. Mostly, I was sad that Tonya let herself get involved in the plot. She's very talented and, even though most skaters never felt they knew her well, I think we all respected her ability. And it was because of that ability that I wondered why I needed to be out of the way. Why not just go out and do what you can do? Why not just skate as well as you are capable of skating and let the judges decide who wins?

We were finally going to get around to doing just that. The longer we were in Norway, the more anxious I was for that day to come. My experiences at the 1994 Olympics were entirely different than they had been two years earlier at the Winter Games in France. Then, I really felt like I was part of the whole U.S. team. In Norway, I sometimes felt like a sideshow in a circus. All of my practices were attended by packs of reporters and photographers, and their numbers only increased after Tonya arrived. Under Olympic rules, we had to practice in the same group every day because we were both competing for the U.S. Fortunately, both of us had been skating for so many years that we knew how to go onto the ice and really concentrate on why we were out there.

The time away from practice actually was more difficult for me. Even though I had quite a bit of privacy at the athletes' village, where the press was not permitted to enter, I sometimes felt as if I couldn't get away from being the center of attention. When I tried to have a meal in the athletes' village dining hall, hoping to blend in with everybody else,

I felt like a freak. Nobody meant any harm, but I sometimes saw athletes from other countries sneaking a peek from around a corner. It felt weird and I wanted to stand up and shout, "What are you looking at? I'm just trying to eat my dinner."

I never encountered Tonya in the dining hall, but I did pass her one day walking through the village. We said hello to each other. I spoke first, wanting to get it over with, and added something about how we'd both had a rough month. Then we went our separate ways. It was really not a conversation and not too comfortable. At that point, I don't know how it could have been comfortable for either one of us.

Finally, the night of the short program competition arrived. I was a little tense, of course, but that was nothing out of the ordinary. I was so prepared and knew there was nothing to fear. I opened my program with a triple lutz–double toe loop jump combination and settled into a groove. With that one important combination over and done with, I had to perform seven more required elements. Everything just clicked after that, and I came off the ice knowing I was on my way. Most of my marks were between 5.7 and 5.9. At the end of the night I was in first place, trailed by Oksana Baiul, the Ukrainian teenager who won the World Championships the year before. Tonya was tenth and now had virtually no chance to win even a bronze medal.

After all of those trying weeks, it was going to come down to a little more than four minutes on a Friday night in Norway. I never felt more ready as I slipped into a shimmering beige dress and went out to warm up with the five other skaters in the final group. Chen Lu of China skated first and her performance later earned her the bronze medal. I was next. My opening jump, a triple flip, didn't feel quite right and I settled for a double. But there was no panic, no sense of trouble looming. I just needed to settle down, which I did just in time to land a pair of triple toe loops in combination. That was a major hurdle and now it was behind me. I could feel a surge of confidence racing through me as I landed jump after jump, just as if I were home doing a run-through with no one around.

Except for the first jump, everything came together as I had hoped and the judges rewarded me with high marks of 5.8 and 5.9. Oksana skated next and proved to be a very determined sixteen-year-old. She, too, avoided serious mistakes and earned equally high marks. The final order of finish was decided by one judge, Jan Hoffman of Germany, a former skater and 1980 Olympic silver medalist. His first place mark to Oksana gave her a total of five judges, while I was rated first by the other four. She became the youngest Olympic skating champion since 1928. I was awarded the silver medal.

Because I have always been a competitor, I was disappointed to miss the gold medal on such a narrow decision. I think it's only natural to hope for the best when you have skated so well in one of the most important nights of an entire career.

But as time went by, I realized that making it to the Olympics so soon after what had happened to me in Detroit was a victory in itself. I had done two of the best programs of my life in Norway. I believed in myself and, when it really mattered, I didn't crack under the pressure. I'll always be proud of that.

Throughout my competitive skating career—and especially in 1994—I discovered that adversity or discouragement only makes me want to work harder. That determination and spirit has to come from deep inside, and my experiences taught me how mentally and physically strong I'm capable of being. Now the voice inside my head says: *Anything is possible.*

It's possible for a tomboy from Massachusetts to grow up and become a women's figure skating champion. It's possible to feel the warmth and positive energy from cheering audiences in small towns and big cities. And it's even possible to find yourself at the Winter Olympics, as millions watch all over the world, skating with a sense of freedom and confidence that comes from the heart.

A Letter from Nancy

THE 1992 AND 1994 Winter Olympics were very important events in my life, but of course my story continues. As a professional skater, I've been able to see a different side of skating. I've become more involved in the business of ice shows and videos. And I've continued competing, which helps me continue to improve as a skater.

Soon after the Olympics, I was off on a three-month, seventy-city journey with the Campbell's Soups Tour of World Champions, featuring many of the best-known skating stars of the 1980s and 1990s. In 1994 I also was the headliner of my own tour, which stopped in a dozen U.S. cities.

I've also competed in "Ice Wars," a new professional skating event featuring a U.S. team and a world team. As more professional competitions are created, I'm sure to continue training, performing, and competing in the years to come.

In addition, I've had the chance to do other exciting projects, like coproduce the *Halloween on Ice* special that aired on TV in 1995. I was involved in designing the costumes and sets, choreographing the routines, and choosing the music.

I also helped with set and costume design and music selection in a series of skating videos based on fairy tales such as "Sleeping Beauty" and "Alice Through the Looking Glass." This was fun because I got to play fairy-tale characters that I read about as I was growing up.

More importantly, my post-Olympic life has put me in a position to help others. I've worked closely with Lions Club International, a large civic organization that supports worthy causes, and I've become involved with a Lions Club project called Campaign SightFirst on a local level.

On a personal level, I got married in the fall of 1995. The wedding was wonderful—it was definitely a highlight of my life! I look forward to having a family and the kind of life outside skating that I've always dreamed about. I've always known that I'm more than just a skater; now I'm excited about exploring those other sides of life.

As I've traveled around the United States, I've met thousands of children, many too young to know what they'll be interested in doing a few years down the road. But I think anyone can succeed at whatever they decide to try. There is excellence in all of us just waiting to come out.

Remember: Anything is possible!